DK READERS

Pre-level 1

Fishy Tales
Colorful Days
Garden Friends
Party Fun
In the Park
Farm Animals
Petting Zoo
Let's Make Music
Meet the Dinosaurs
Duck Pond Dip
My Dress-up Box

On the Move
Snakes Slither and Hiss
Family Vacation
Ponies and Horses
My Day
Monkeys
Big Trucks
John Deere: Busy Tractors
Lego Duplo: On the Farm
Cuentos de Peces en *español*
Dias Ilenos de color en *español*

Level 1

A Day at Greenhill Farm
Truck Trouble
Tale of a Tadpole
Surprise Puppy!
Duckling Days
A Day at Seagull Beach
Whatever the Weather
Busy Buzzy Bee
Big Machines
Wild Baby Animals
A Bed for the Winter
Born to be a Butterfly
Dinosaur's Day
Feeding Time
Diving Dolphin
Rockets and Spaceships
My Cat's Secret
First Day at Gymnastics
A Trip to the Zoo
I Can Swim!
A Trip to the Library
A Trip to the Doctor
A Trip to the Dentist
I Want to be a Ballerina
Animal Hide and Seek
Submarines and Submersibles
Animals at Home
Let's Play Soccer
Homes Around the World

Bugs and Us
Train Travel
LEGO: Trouble at the Bridge
LEGO: Secret at Dolphin Bay
Star Wars: What is a Wookie?
Star Wars: Ready, Set, Podrace!
Star Wars: Luke Skywalker's Amazing
   Story
Star Wars Clone Wars: Watch Out for
   Jabba the Hutt!
Star Wars Clone Wars: Pirates... and
   Worse
Power Rangers: Jungle Fury: We are the
   Power Rangers
Lego Duplo: Around Town
Indiana Jones: Indy's Adventures
John Deere: Good Morning, Farm!
A Day in the Life of a Builder
A Day in the Life of a Dancer
A Day in the Life of a Firefighter
A Day in the Life of a Teacher
A Day in the Life of a Musician
A Day in the Life of a Doctor
A Day in the Life of a Police Officer
A Day in the Life of a TV Reporter
Gigantes de Hierro en *español*
Crías del mundo animal en *español*

A Note to Parents

DK READERS is a compelling program for beginning readers, designed in conjunction with leading literacy experts, including Dr. Linda Gambrell, Distinguished Professor of Education at Clemson University. Dr. Gambrell has served as President of the National Reading Conference, the College Reading Association, and the International Reading Association.

Beautiful illustrations and superb full-color photographs combine with engaging, easy-to-read stories to offer a fresh approach to each subject in the series. Each DK READER is guaranteed to capture a child's interest while developing his or her reading skills, general knowledge, and love of reading.

The five levels of DK READERS are aimed at different reading abilities, enabling you to choose the books that are exactly right for your child:

Pre-level 1: Learning to read
Level 1: Beginning to read
Level 2: Beginning to read alone
Level 3: Reading alone
Level 4: Proficient readers

The "normal" age at which a child begins to read can be anywhere from three to eight years old. Adult participation through the lower levels is very helpful for providing encouragement, discussing storylines, and sounding out unfamiliar words.

No matter which level you select, you can be sure that you are helping your child learn to read, then read to learn!

LONDON, NEW YORK, MUNICH,
MELBOURNE, AND DELHI

DK LONDON
Series Editor Deborah Lock
Art Director Martin Wilson
Production Editor Francesca Wardell
Jacket Designer Martin Wilson
Reading Consultant
Linda Gambrell, Ph.D

DK DELHI
Senior Editor Priyanka Nath
Senior Art Editor Rajnish Kashyap
Assistant Editor Deeksha Saikia
Assistant Designer Tanvi Sahu
DTP Designer Anita Yadav
Picture Researcher Sumedha Chopra

First American Edition, 2013
Published in the United States by DK Publishing
375 Hudson Street, New York, New York 10014

13 14 15 16 17 10 9 8 7 6 5 4 3 2 1
001—187464—June/2013

DK books are available at special discounts when purchased in bulk for sales
promotions, premiums, fund-raising, or educational use.

For details, contact: DK Publishing Special Markets
375 Hudson Street, New York, New York 10014
SpecialSales@dk.com

A catalog record for this book is available from the Library of Congress.

ISBN: 978-1-46540-890-7 (Paperback)
ISBN: 978-1-46540-891-4 (Hardcover)

Color reproduction by Colourscan, Singapore
Printed and bound in China by L Rex Printing Co., Ltd.

Discover more at
www.dk.com

Contents

4 Trucks

8 Flatbed trucks

10 Tow trucks

12 Big rigs

14 Road rollers

16 Forklift trucks

18 Diggers

20 Wheel loaders

22 Dump trucks

24 Excavators

26 Compactors

28 Fire trucks

30 Monster trucks

32 Glossary

DK **READERS**

LEARNING TO READ — pre-level 1

Big Trucks

DK Publishing

Trucks are BIG.

Trucks are heavy.

Trucks pull and carry loads.

The truck carries goods along the road.

goods

trucks

cab

7

The flatbed truck carries loads on its trailer.

trailer

flatbed trucks

load

The tow truck carries a broken-down car.

boom ⎯

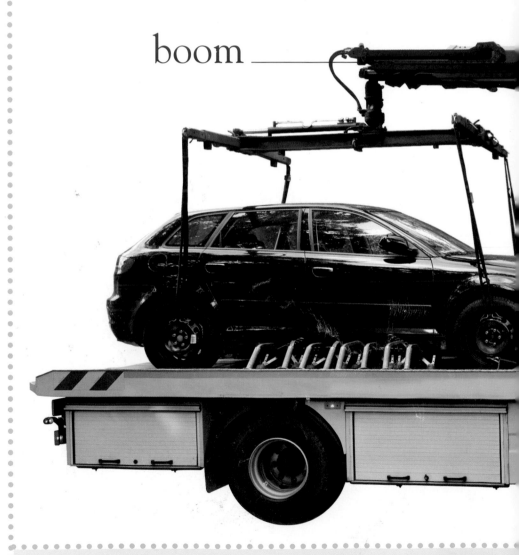

tow trucks

tow
hitch

11

exhaust

big rigs

The big rig pulls
many trailers
on long trips.

trailer

13

The heavy road roller flattens the road.

road rollers

drum roller

The forklift truck moves the loads.

load

 forklift trucks

driver

fork

17

The digger will lift the rubble in its bucket.

bucket

diggers

rubble

The wheel loader scoops up large rocks.

wheel loaders

bucket

rock

21

The dump truck tips up its back so the rubble slides out.

open-box bed

dump trucks

22

cab

The excavator digs trenches with its shovel.

excavators

caterpillar track

shovel

trench

The compactor
presses down with
its spiked wheels.

compactors

26

spiked
wheel

The fire trucks have hoses and ladders to help put out fires.

ladder _____.

fire trucks

28

_____ hose

The monster truck does stunts on its huge wheels.

monster trucks

hood

wheel

Glossary

Compactor
a machine that squashes waste or soil into smaller amounts

Excavator
a machine that has a cab and bucket on a turning platform

Forklift truck
a truck that lifts and moves loads

Monster truck
a pickup truck with very large wheels for doing stunts

Wheel loader
a machine with a bucket to dig out earth and rocks

Index